THE Self Care & EMPOWERMENT

COLORING BOOK FOR WOMEN & GIRLS

instagram: @MarieRiversColoring

facebook.com/MarieRiversColoring

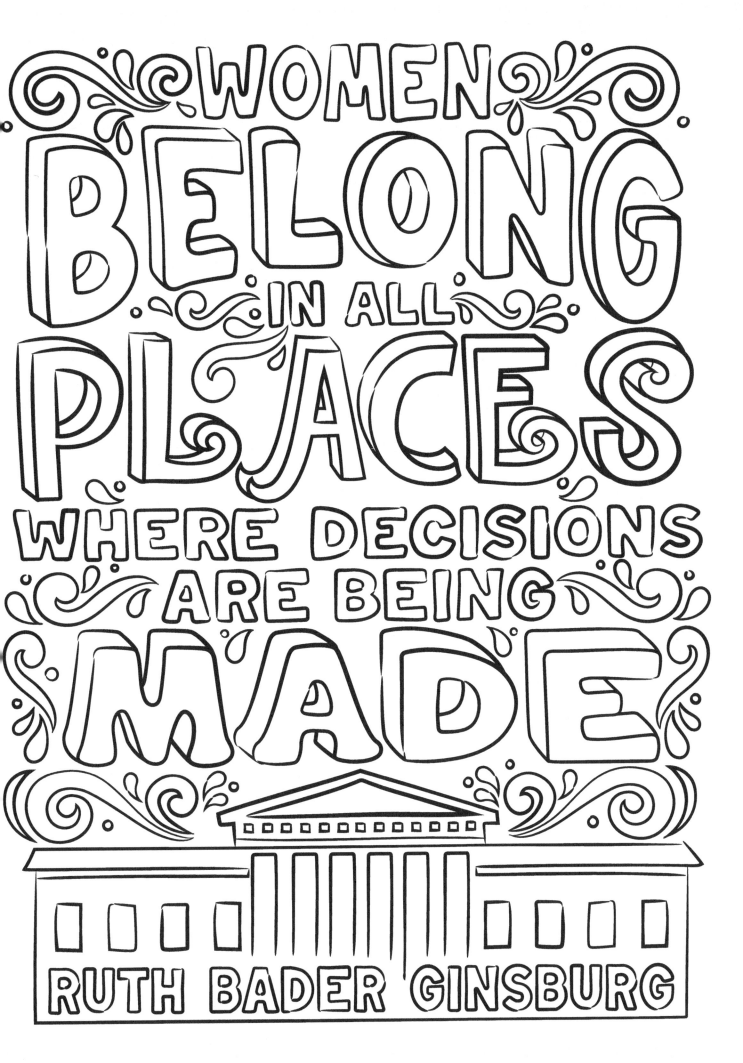

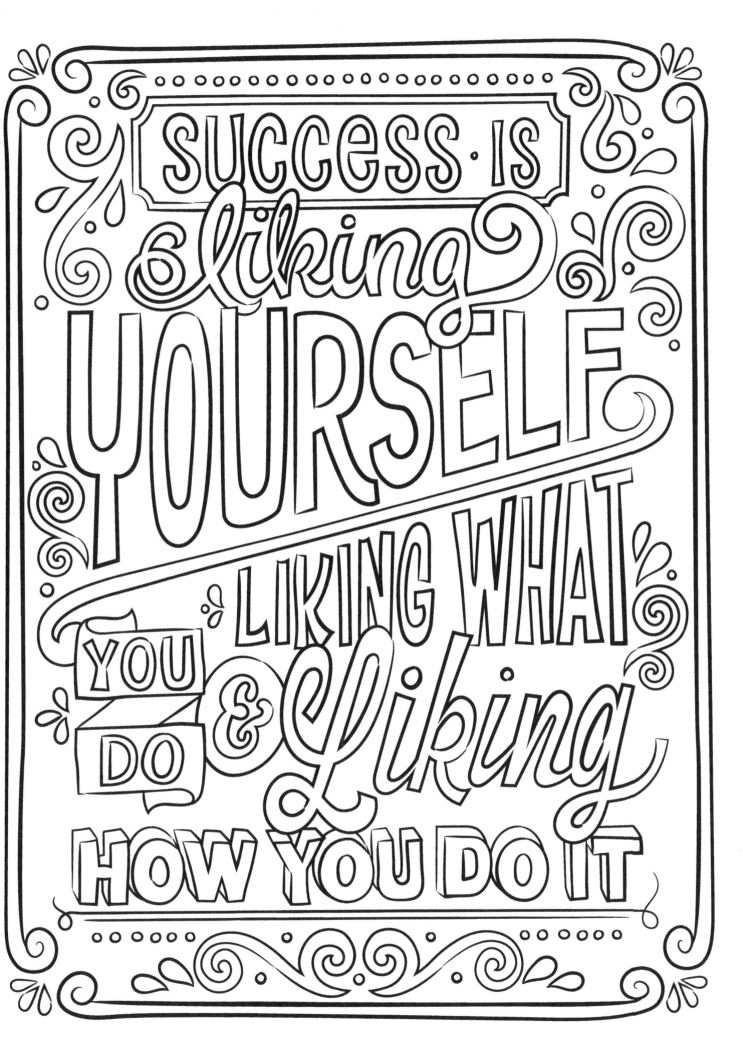

BE CURIOUS NOT judgemental

WALT WHITMAN

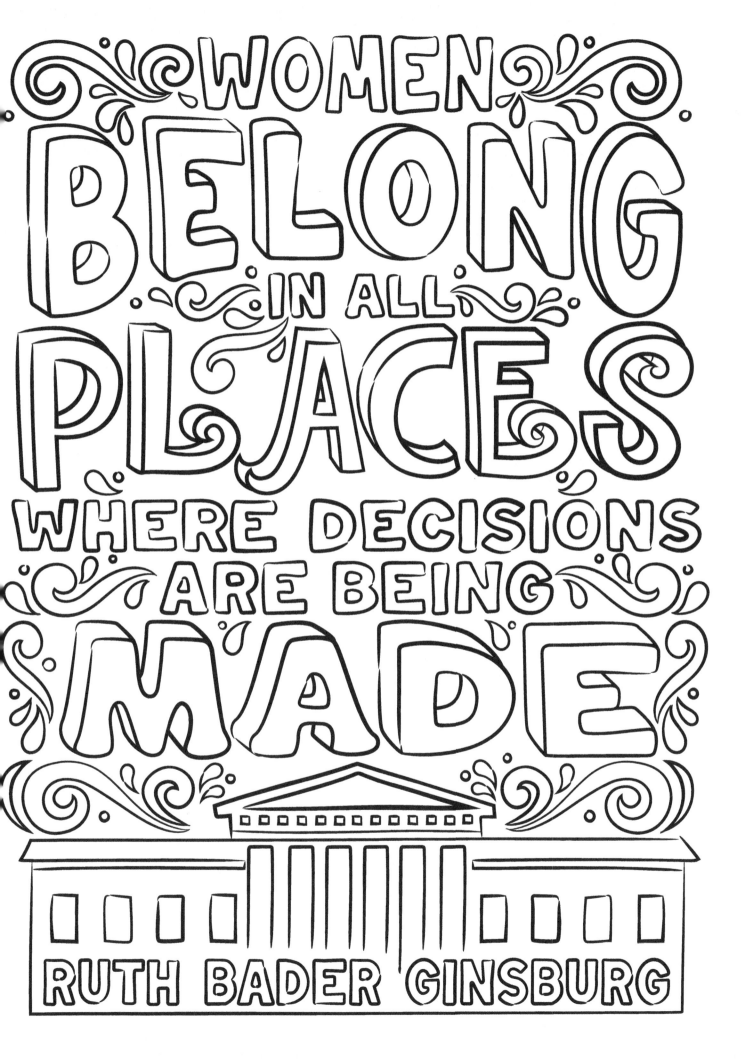

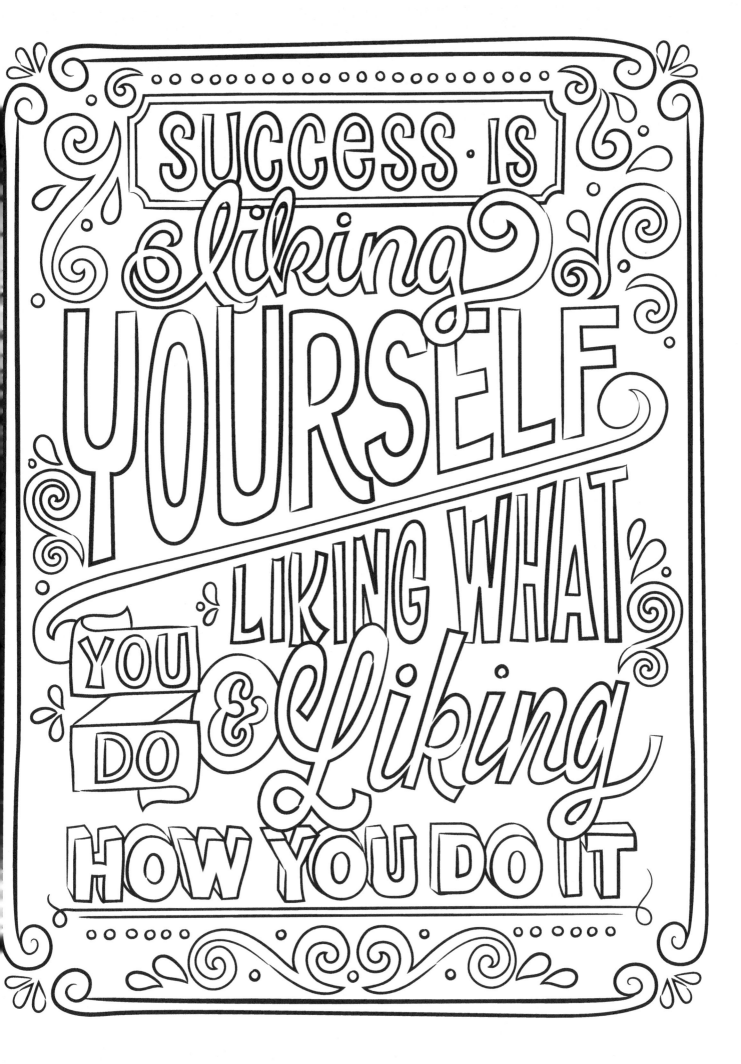

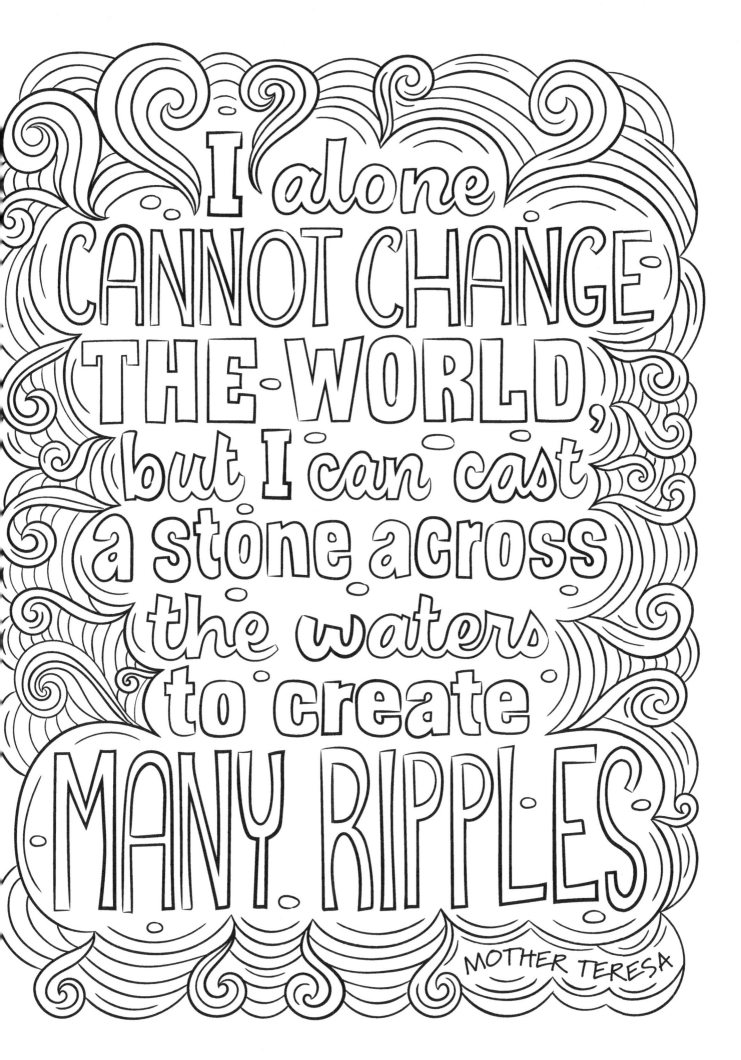

BE CURIOUS NOT judgemental

WALT WHITMAN

FOLD

Focus on what you think not of you

Self Care

Made in the USA
Middletown, DE
05 March 2020